MW01006489

Breaking *Family* CURSES

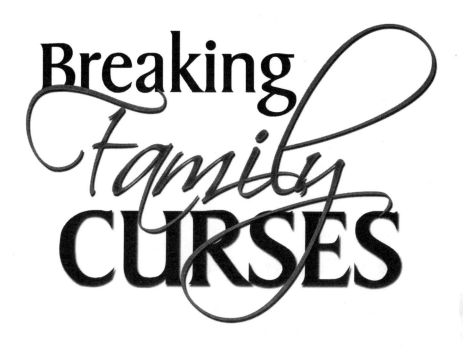

Jonas Clark

Unless otherwise noted, Scripture quotations are taken from the King James Version of the Bible.

Breaking Family Curses
ISBN-10: 1-886885-49-4
ISBN-13: 978-1-886885-49-3

Published by Spirit of Life Publishing
27 West Hallandale Beach Blvd.
Hallandale, Florida
33009-5437, U.S.A.
(954) 456-4420

www.JonasClark.com

Printed in India

02 03 04 05 06 07 ¨ 07 06 05 04 03 02

ABOUT THE AUTHOR

The anointing on Jonas Clark's life is both strong and bold. His great passion is to equip believers to invade, occupy, influence, and establish Kingdom of God culture through the power of the Gospel of Jesus Christ.

Jonas has been in global ministry for over thirty years, written more than 55 books, and preached in more than 30 nations. He is the founder of Spirit of Life Ministries in Hallandale Beach, FL, the Global Cause Network of apostolic and prophetic remnant believers, and the Apostolic Equipping Institute with students in more than 60 nations.

This Book is Dedicated to....

all praying parents, grandparents and children
who are believing for deliverance and freedom
from family curses. I am praying with you.
— *Jonas Clark*

CONTENTS

INTRODUCTION

Demon powers and familiar spirits look for family curses. Family curses are reoccurring problems that steal, kill, and destroy. There are many curses that can plague you from reoccurring sicknesses, marital problems, to repeated financial failures. Curses can visit because of relatives up your family tree because God visits the iniquities of the fathers upon the children to the third and fourth generation.

You cannot choose your relatives anymore than you can choose skin color, gender, or race. Did someone in your family lineage sin against God? Could it be possible that family curses were passed down your family tree? Mature believers don't let the demons of family members past alter their futures.

It is comforting to know that deliverance from family curses belongs to you. Before you can break generational curses you need to identify what they look like. Family curses are real. You can't hide from them, you must break them. In this book learn the easy way to stop them from attacking your life, family and ministry. You have nothing to lose but your chains.

Your partner,

Jonas Clark
www.jonasclark.com

Chapter 1

WHAT HAPPENS IN VEGAS?

Some say what happens in Vegas stays in Vegas. That sounds like an invitation for sin. Sin, however, affects you, your family and your family descendants. Sin, no matter the location, opens the door for family curses. Family curses are reoccurring problems that steal, kill, and destroy.

There are many family curses that plague from repeated sicknesses, marital problems, to financial failures.

If you go to a medical doctor for an examination they will ask you for your family's medical history. They do that because they know certain diseases reoccur within family lines. It's the same for generational curses.

The honest person must ask himself how a Christian can suffer from a curse. The short answer is ignorance. For example, most Christians believe that healing belongs to them through the atoning blood of Christ. Scripture confirms this belief declaring, "By His stripes ye are healed" (1 Peter 2:24). There are thousands of examples of Christians receiving healing in their bodies after salvation. It is evident, however, that other Christians are sick. If healing belongs to them then why are they suffering sickness? The answer is that healing has already been provided but they have yet to experience it. Another scripture says, "Faith cometh by hearing and hearing by the Word" (Romans 10:17).

To appropriate anything from the Lord one must know what belongs to them and receive it by faith. The same goes for deliverance from family curses.

The word salvation is the Greek word *sozo*. "For by grace are ye saved (sozo) through faith; and that not of yourselves: it is the gift of God" (Ephesians 2:8). Sozo can also translate as deliverance. Jesus spoke of deliverance. He said the Spirit of the Lord was on Him because he was anointed to preach deliverance to the captives. Deliverance is the children's bread (Matthew 15:22-28). It belongs to you through the will of Christ. He is the one that "went about doing good and healing all that were sick and oppressed of the devil for God was with him" (Acts 10:38). It is not until a believer knows what belongs to him or her can faith for that promise be received.

It is comforting to know that deliverance from family curses belongs to you. Freedom has already been promised. Scripture declares, "Christ hath redeemed us from the curse of the law, being made a curse for us: for it is written, Cursed is every one that hangeth on a tree" (Galatians 3:13). Redeemed means the recompense for sin and iniquities has already been paid for by the atoning blood of the only begotten Son of God. So as we discuss freedom from family curses in this essay read it with the assurance that deliverance has already been provided to those that receive Christ' redemption by faith.

INIQUITY OF THE FATHERS

Scripture is clear that God visits the iniquity of the fathers upon the children. These are oftentimes referred as generational curses. I want to use the term family

5

curses to explain. Here is one of our foundational verses for understanding the source of family curses.

> "Thou shalt not bow down thyself to them, nor serve them: for I the Lord thy God am a jealous God, visiting the iniquity of the fathers upon the children unto the third and fourth generation of them that hate me." (Exodus 20:5)

Notice it is iniquity that God visits upon the family tree of the disobedient. Iniquity is unjust acts, wickedness, amoral behavior, idolatry, sexual sins, rebellion, witchcraft, evil, and mischief. All of us have parents, four grandparents, eight great-grandparents, and sixteen great-great-grandparents. That's a total of thirty two relatives in our family tree. Could it be possible a family curse was passed down the family line because of one of them?

THE KENNEDY CURSE

The Kennedy family curse has been well documented. Wikipedia writes:

> The Kennedy tragedies, colloquially called the Kennedy Curse, is a term sometimes used to describe a series of tragedies involving members

of the Kennedy family. Some have called the continual misfortune of the Kennedy family a curse. Several members of the family have died from unnatural causes, most notably brothers John and Robert, who were assassinated by gunshots in 1963 and 1968, and John, Jr., who was killed in an airplane crash along with his wife and sister-in-law in 1999.

The existence of such a curse has been disputed by others who have claimed that many of the tragedies have been caused by preventable reckless choices like driving drunk or flying an airplane in unsafe conditions, that others are the natural result of events likely to occur in such a large family like cancer or pregnancy miscarriage, and that the notion of a curse is superstitious and created and fostered by the media.

The last Kennedy family member to suffer was John F. Kennedy, Jr. John was the oldest and only surviving son of President Kennedy and was killed in a plane crash along with his wife and sister-in-law off the coast of Martha's Vineyard July 16, 1999. This was a national tragedy bringing back more discussion of the possibility of a Kennedy family curse.

THE LEE FAMILY CURSE

Many remember the martial arts master known as Bruce Lee. Lee was born Lee Jun-fan. He is considered one of the most influential martial artists of the 20th century, and a cultural icon. Lee was born in San Francisco, California in the United States, to parents of Hong Kong heritage but raised in Hong Kong until his late teens. Upon reaching the age of 18, Lee emigrated to the United States to claim his U.S. Citizenship and receive a higher education. It was during this time he began teaching martial arts, which soon led to film and television roles.

One night he took some medication for a simple headache. Sometime later he suffered a serious allergic reaction causing a cerebral edema. He died at the early age of 32. A month later his classic kung fu move *"Enter the Dragon"* was released.

Twenty years later his only son Brandon Lee was working on a movie called *"The Crow"* about a rock musician revived from the dead to avenge his own murder. During the final days of filming his character was to be shot. The day before a props team member mistook a "squib load", a real bullet in the barrel. The next day another props team loaded the gun with blanks but when the gun was fired it had enough gunpowder to fire the squib load killing the 28-year-old Lee. Like his father, Brandon Lee died young. This was also reported in the media as a family curse.

THE BRANDO FAMILY CURSE

Marlon Brando, Jr. was named the fourth greatest male star of all time by the American Film Institute, and part of *Time* magazine's "Time 100: The Most Important People of the Century." He was perhaps best known for his roles as Stanley Kowalski in "*A Streetcar Named Desire*" (1951) and his Academy Award-winning performance as Terry Malloy in "*On the Waterfront*" (1954), both directed by Elia Kazan, and his Academy Award-winning performance as Vito Corleone in Francis Ford Coppola's "*The Godfather*" (1972). In middle age he also played Colonel Walter Kurtz in "*Apocalypse Now*" (1979) and delivered an Academy Award-nominated performance as Paul in "*Last Tango in Paris*" (1972).

Brando's mother suffered from alcoholism, and his first wife, Anna Kashfi, developed drug and alcohol problems after giving birth to their son Christian. Along with his own drug problems, Christian shot the boyfriend of his half-sister Cheyenne. Dag Drollet, the Tahitian lover of Brando's daughter Cheyenne, died of a gunshot wound after a confrontation with Cheyenne's half-brother Christian at the family's hilltop home above Beverly Hills. Christian, then 31 years old, claimed he was drunk and the shooting was accidental. He was convicted of voluntary manslaughter and served six years of his ten-year sentence.

In an effort to prevent Cheyenne from testifying at Christian's trial, Marlon Brando sent her to Tahiti so she couldn't be subpoenaed by U.S. authorities. A year before Christian was released, she committed suicide. Christian Brando died of pneumonia at age 49.

These are three examples of family curses discussed in American newspapers. There have been many more including the Hemingway, Barrymore, and Redgrave families. Some would say this is just plain superstition and think nothing of it. Others, however, might want to think a little more about it especially when they see signs of family curses within their own families. If anything these stories make us question the possibility of real family curses and ask if there is a way of escape. Even though these accounts are saddening the good news is that family curses do not have to continue, they can be stopped.

THE RECOMPENSE FOR INIQUITY

Curses come on families because of sin and disobedience to the Word of God. They are the results of rebellion. Our God is a God of covenant. He is a God of law and the judge of all. Every covenant has sanctions. Without sanctions there is no covenant. Sanctions are penalties or other means of enforcement used to provide incentives for obedience with the law, or with rules and regulations. Just as the Bible is full of blessings for obedience there are also penalties when laws are broken. These penalties we call family curses.

A curse is a payment or "recompense for iniquity."

> "Render unto them a recompense, o Lord, according to the work of their hands. Give them sorrow of heart, thy curse unto them. Persecute and destroy them in anger from under the heavens of the Lord." (Lamentations 3:64-66)

Sin has consequences. Scripture declares "For the wages of sin is death; but the gift of God is eternal life through Jesus Christ our Lord" (Romans 6:23). Recompense can come as failure, premature death, sickness, diseases, destruction, tragedy, marriage problems, mental illness, suicide, torment, depression, sorrow, grief, lack, hopelessness, confusion, guilt, shame, setbacks, accidents, addictions, reprobate minds, sexual perversions, whoredoms, vagabondism, barrenness, lack, female problems, and fear.

IT DOESN'T STAY IN VEGAS

Las Vegas is known as Sin City. Perhaps you have heard the official Las Vegas tourism slogan "What happens in Vegas, stays in Vegas." Not so when it comes to the repercussions of sin and iniquities flowing down the family line. Scripture says,

> "Moreover all these curses shall come upon thee, and shall pursue thee, and overtake thee, till thou be destroyed; because thou hearkenedst not unto the voice of the Lord thy God, to keep his commandments and his statutes which he commanded thee" (Deuteronomy 28:45).

One may sin in Vegas but the results of those sins never stay in Vegas. You can run but you can't hide. That's because curses pursue and overtake. As we have already discovered disobedience opens the door for family curses, and the recompense for iniquities. These curses can enter through generational curses, sin, fantasy, pornography, unforgiveness, rape, drugs, witchcraft, sexual perversion, serving others gods, and rebellion.

THE JUKES FAMILY

Sociologist Richard L. Dugdale wrote "*The Jukes: A Study in Crime, Pauperism, Disease and Heredity*" in 1877. He was a member of the executive committee of the Prison Association of New York that was delegated to visit jails in upstate New York. In a jail in Ulster County he found six members of the same family and recorded their family history. According to his research he claimed to have traced the family's Hudson Valley roots back seven generations to a colonial frontiersman named Max, whom he described as having been born between 1720 and 1740, a descendant of early Dutch settlers, who lived in the backwoods as a "hunter and fisher, a hard drinker, jolly and companionable, averse to steady toil." He traced the branch that had produced so many criminals back to a woman he called "Margaret, the Mother of Criminals," who had married one of Max's sons.

Max Juke and his wife are examples of a family curse. They were godless atheists. They had 560 descendants. 310 died in poverty, 150 were criminals,

100 alcoholics, 7 murders, and more than half the women were prostitutes.

THE EDWARDS FAMILY

Contrast that family tree to the Edwards' family. Jonathan Edwards played a critical role in shaping the First Great Awakening, and oversaw some of the first fires of revival in 1733-1735 at his church in Northampton, Massachusetts. Edwards sermon "Sinners in the Hands of an Angry God," is considered a classic of early American literature, which he delivered during another wave of revival in 1741, following George Whitefield's tour of the Thirteen Colonies.

Jonathan Edwards and wife were committed Christians. Of their 1394 descendants, 294 were college graduates, 13 college presidents, 30 judges, 65 college professors, 75 military officers, 100 missionaries, 100 lawyers, 80 held public office, 3 were U. S. Senators, 3 State Governors, 3 Mayors, 1 Comptroller of the U. S. Treasury and 1 Vice-president of the United States.

The differences between the Juke and Edwards' family trees are eye opening. God's word is clear, "The wicked are overthrown and are not but the house of the righteous shall stand" (Proverbs 12:7). The bottom line is that the wages of sin is death. What happens in Vegas, does not stay in Vegas, it follows down the family lineage.

Before you can break family curses we need to identify what they look like. In the next chapter discover seven signs of a family curse.

Chapter 2

7 SIGNS OF
A FAMILY CURSE

F amily curses are reoccurring problems that steal, kill, and destroy. Scripture is clear God visits the iniquity of the fathers upon the children up to the third and fourth generation (Exodus 20:5). Curses don't visit your family without a cause. When someone up the family tree gives spirits the right to visit because of iniquity they come looking for a reason to mess up your life. Take courage. After family curses are exposed Christ's deliverance is readily available.

You cannot choose your relatives anymore than you can choose skin color, gender, or race. Someone up the family tree could be the cause for a generational curse. A family curse is a payment or "recompense for iniquity." It is written,

> "Render unto them a recompense, o Lord, according to the work of their hands. Give them sorrow of heart, thy curse unto them. Persecute and destroy them in anger from under the heavens of the Lord" (Lamentations 3:64-66).

Before you can break generational curses we need to identify what they look like. Here is a partial list of family curses for your review. Having one of these in your life or family may not indicate a family curse. To have several "reoccurring" ones might. The help of the Holy Spirit is vital in identifying a family curse. As you read this list ask Him to give you a spirit of revelation.

1. EMOTIONAL INSTABILITY, FEAR

> "The Lord shall smite thee with madness, and blindness, and astonishment of heart." (Deuteronomy 28:28)

The first curse we will discuss is emotional instability. Notice the Scripture above says the Lord will "smite with madness." To be smitten with madness means insanity, craziness, foolishness, senseless behavior, and flakiness. He also uses the term "blindness." This blindness releases confusion, indecision, and wonderment.

If that's not enough God follows that with "astonishment of heart" meaning a trembling, unsettled, and fearful heart.

Under this curse one is easily overcome by emotions and fear. These trigger a person to make foolish decisions and do crazy self-destructive things. In this condition a person has a continual inner struggle, internal warfare, and frustration.

Confusion and depression are two key indicators of this family curse. This curse teaches why some are double-minded and have problems ordering their lives with the word of God and renewing their minds.

2. HEREDITARY SICKNESSES

"The Lord shall make the pestilence cleave unto thee, until he have consumed thee from off the land, whither thou goest to possess it. The Lord shall smite thee with a consumption, and with a fever, and with an inflammation, and with an extreme burning, and with the sword, and with blasting, and with mildew; and they shall pursue thee until thou perish." (Deuteronomy 28:21)

Some family sicknesses are reoccurring. Reoccurring is the indication of a family curse. Notice the terms "pestilence" and "consumption."

This curse releases sicknesses of all kinds. Consumption is a wasting lung disease, infazema, COPD, and lung cancer. Lung cancer is the number three killer.

He also uses terms, "fever" and "inflammation." These indicate a curse that is evidenced by arthritis. Inflammation of the brain leads to Alzheimer disease. Then we read the term "extreme burning." Extreme burning means all sorts of strange fevers.

THE BOTCH

"The Lord will smite thee with the botch of Egypt, and with the emerods, and with the scab, and with the itch, whereof thou canst not be healed." (Deuteronomy 28:27)

The botches are open sores or boils. These can be experienced by those that have problems with wounds that will not heal. Scripture also says,

"The Lord shall smite thee in the knees, and in the legs, with a sore botch that cannot be healed, from the sole of thy foot unto the top of thy head" (Deuteronomy 28:35).

This curse attacks legs, soles of the feet, and the top of one's head. The Lord didn't leave any diseases out of this curse. He declared,

"Also every sickness, and every plague, which is not written in the book of this law, them will the Lord bring upon thee, until thou be destroyed." (Deuteronomy 28:61)

3. BARRENNESS, IMPOTENCE, FEMALE PROBLEMS

"Cursed shall be the fruit of thy body, and the fruit of thy land, the increase of thy kine, and the flocks of thy sheep." (Deuteronomy 28:18)

Perhaps you have heard menstrual problems known as "the curse." Sometimes folklore comes from biblical tradition. Menstrual problems may be the result of a family curse. Scripture says, "Cursed shall be the fruit of thy body." The word body, Hebrew *beten*, means womb, belly, or abdomen. The womb deals with reproduction. Signs of this curse are infections, hormone problems, menstrual problems, PMS, cramps, fibroids, painful sex, barrenness, miscarriages, cysts, tumors, bladder problems and kidney stones. Female problems plague millions of women. Men too can manifest this curse with erectile dysfunction and impotence.

4. FAMILY BREAKDOWNS, DIVORCE

This curse manifest in several ways including divorce, family divides, fights among relatives, families that scatter, no fellowship, jailed children and estranged relationships.

> "Thou shalt betroth a wife, and another man shall lie with her: thou shalt build an house, and thou shalt not dwell therein: thou shalt plant a vineyard, and shalt not gather the grapes thereof." (Deuteronomy 28:30)

The divorce rate in America is 50 percent for first marriages, 67 percent for second marriages, and 74%

for third marriages according to the Forest Institute of Professional Psychology.

Children are also affected by this family curse.

"Thy sons and thy daughters shall be given unto another people, and thine eyes shall look, and fail with longing for them all the day long: and there shall be no might in thine hand." (Deuteronomy 28:32)

"Thou shalt beget sons and daughters, but thou shalt not enjoy them; for they shall go into captivity." (Deuteronomy 28:41)

The iniquities of the fathers are visited on the children. Here are the stats of family breakdowns affecting children:

- 1.2 million children are born in fatherless homes.

- 1.8 million children are latch key kids.

- 36 percent of kids grow up without a father.
- 75 percent of kids on drugs

come from single parent homes.

- 63 percent of youth suicides
  come from single parent homes.

- 70 percent of teen pregnancies
  come from single parent homes.

- 75 percent of jailed juveniles
  come from single parent homes.

5. LACK, POVERTY, INABILITY TO PRODUCE

"Cursed shall be thy basket and thy store (kneading trough)." (Deuteronomy 28:17)

"And thou shalt grope at noonday, as the blind gropeth in darkness, and thou shalt not prosper in thy ways: and thou shalt be only oppressed and spoiled evermore, and no man shall save thee." (Deuteronomy 28:29)

This is a curse on finances. A kneading trough is where food is prepared. I liken this to the ability to produce. Production is the vehicle toward wealth building. Under this curse one's ability to get wealth is stopped. People under this curse never have anything saved. They are continually oppressed by bill collectors and what little they accumulate is stolen by the spoilers (Judges 2:14).

DEBTORS

These same people are slaves to their creditors. Scripture declares,

> "Because thou servedst not the Lord thy God with joyfulness, and with gladness of heart, for the abundance of all things; Therefore shalt thou serve thine enemies which the Lord shall send against thee, in hunger, and in thirst, and in nakedness, and in want of all things: and he shall put a yoke of iron upon thy neck, until he have destroyed thee." (Deuteronomy 28:47-48)

This family curse of lack and poverty needs to be broken as God's promise says, "And God is able to make all grace abound toward you; that ye, always having all sufficiency in all things, may abound to every good work" (2 Corinthians 9:8).

Poverty is not having what you need to do God's will. It is not the blessing of God to not have the means to accomplish His plan for your life. A person under this curse will squander, waste and get further in debt and bondage. They are candidates for get-rich schemes of all kinds. The blessed man is not focused on material wealth but on fulfilling their purpose in life as they keep and follow the commandments of the Lord putting first the Kingdom of God and His righteousness (Matthew 6:33).

6. NO AMBITION, VISION, DIRECTION

"And thou shalt grope at noonday, as the blind gropeth in darkness, and thou shalt not prosper in thy ways: and thou shalt be only oppressed and spoiled evermore, and no man shall save thee." (Deuteronomy 28:29)

I have met those that have no internal vision for their lives. They set no goals and are blown to and fro by lives circumstances. This curse is revealed in those without ambition. They go aimlessly through life. Ambition is a strong desire to make a difference with your life. It's a vision, dream, or aspiration to succeed. Those under this curse care less about tomorrow. They are without hope and terribly negative. They "grope" as "blind men" with no direction, constantly uncertain and full of apathy and lukewarmness.

7. BONDAGE AND SLAVERY

"The stranger that is within thee shall get up above thee very high; and thou shalt come down very low. He shall lend to thee, and thou shalt not lend to him: he shall be the head, and thou shalt be the tail." (Deuteronomy 28:43-44)

This person loses his individualism, liberty and freedom. They are easily controlled and manipulated into loss of identity. They lose their personal liberties, can't make decisions on their own, and must get permission from their masters. This person will look to other gods for provision and protection, not unto the Lord. They are faithless, carnal, and full of idolatry, entertainment, and anything that divides them from the lordship of Christ.

Knowing that God visits the iniquity of the fathers upon the children up to the third and fourth generation has been quite a shocker for some. You have learned however that curses don't visit the family without a cause. Someone up the family tree could have been the originator. Breaking family curses required you to think about what reoccurring things attack the family. By now we are sure the Holy Spirit has showed you some possibilities. As we progress in this teaching series you will learn how to break family curses. There is much more to come.

A family curse cannot attack without a cause. In the next chapter let's review some biblical examples.

Chapter 3

NO CAUSE NO CURSE

C urses find a cause. Scripture declares, "The curse causeless shall not come" (Proverbs 26:2). In other words something happened that caused them. Family curses are the result of sin or someone in the family rebelling against God's sanctions. These violations bring curses down the family tree because of iniquity.

Family curses come on families because of sin and disobedience to the Word of God. They are released when someone breaks God's laws. Since Jehovah is a God of covenant every covenant has sanctions. Without sanctions there is no covenant. Sanctions are penalties or other means of enforcement used to provide incentives for obedience with the law, or with rules and regulations. The Word is full of blessings for obedience and penalties when scriptural laws are broken. These penalties we call curses. Curses don't come without a cause. Here are six curses that found a cause. As you read these examples keep in mind that Christ shed His blood for the redemption of sin and by His stripes you were healed.

1. CAIN WAS CURSED FOR SHEDDING INNOCENT BLOOD

"And the Lord said unto Cain, Where is Abel thy brother? And he said, I know not: Am I my brother's keeper? And he said, What hast thou done? The voice of thy brother's blood crieth unto me from the ground. And now art thou cursed from the earth, which hath opened her mouth to receive thy brother's blood from thy hand." (Genesis 4:9-11)

Cain murdered his brother Abel because of jealousy. Jehovah would not receive Cain's offering but received the firstlings from Abel. Cain refused to acknowledge the lordship of Jehovah by refusing to tithe. By murdering his brother he cursed himself, left the family of God, and built the first city-state government. This was the birthing of secular humanism, statism, and the division of kingdoms. The ideology of statism holds that sovereignty is vested not in Jehovah God but in the national state, and that all individuals and associations exist only to enhance the power, the prestige, and the well-being of the state. A Christian should never look to the State as their protector-provider. That role belongs to Christ alone (Exodus 20:1-3).

2. CANAAN, NOAH'S GRANDSON, WAS CURSED FOR SEXUAL PERVERSION

"And Noah began to be an husbandman, and he planted a vineyard: And he drank of the wine, and was drunken; and he was uncovered within his tent. And Ham, the father of Canaan, saw the nakedness of his father, and told his two brethren without. And Shem and Japheth took a garment, and laid it upon both their shoulders, and went backward, and covered the nakedness of their father; and their faces were backward, and they saw not their father's nakedness. And Noah awoke from his wine, and knew what his younger son had done unto him. And he said, Cursed be

Canaan; a servant of servants shall he be unto his brethren." (Genesis 9:20-25)

Noah spoke a curse over his grandson Canaan, son of Ham because of sin. It should be clear the iniquity of Ham was transferred down the family tree and affected his family lineage. According to Spiros Zodhiates, editor of *The Key Word Study Bible*,

> "The fact that Noah's curse was directed against Canaan indicates that Canaan was somehow involved in immoral and indecent behavior with his drunken grandfather. Ham was indirectly to blame because he had allowed Canaan to grow up with this character and because he evidently did not treat Noah with respect when he found him."

Noah was the family padrino. His words carried high-level spiritual authority. According to Zodhiates Canaan was cursed because of sexual perversion that was working within his family. Noah's prophecy was fulfilled when the Canaanites became "hewers of wood and drawers of water" for the Israelites (Joshua 9:23). The words from Noah were not out of hatred or malice but spoken out of his spirit. Scripture is clear, "The wages of sin is death." This curse was the result of Ham's sin released down the family tree and manifesting itself in Canaan's actions.

3. BRINGING ABOMINATIONS, MORALLY DISGUSTING OBJECTS OR IDOLS INTO YOUR HOUSE

"The graven images of their gods shall ye burn with fire: thou shalt not desire the silver or gold that is on them, nor take it unto thee, lest thou be snared therein: for it is an abomination to the Lord thy God. Neither shalt thou bring an abomination into thine house, lest thou be a cursed thing like it: but thou shalt utterly detest it, and thou shalt utterly abhor it; for it is a cursed thing." (Deuteronomy 7:25-26)

These items include such perverse things as demonic objects, jewelry, paintings, art, books, music, games, videos, and occult items.

4. REBUILDING WHAT GOD DESTROYED

"And Joshua adjured them at that time, saying, Cursed be the man before the Lord, that riseth up and buildeth this city Jericho: he shall lay the foundation thereof in his firstborn, and in his youngest son shall he set up the gates of it." (Joshua 6:26)

Countless have received forgiveness and freedom from the powers of darkness. Cursed is the man that rebuilds or reintroduces into the lives of others anything the Holy Spirit once destroyed. For example, ungodly soul ties and family curses that were broken by the power of the Spirit, addictions and sexual perversions, or spiritualism and witchcraft. To introduce bondage anew into a person's life brings a curse.

5. OPERATING IN A JEZEBEL SPIRIT BRINGS A CURSE

"And when Jehu was come to Jezreel, Jezebel heard of it; and she painted her face, and tired her head, and looked out at a window. And as Jehu entered in at the gate, she said, Had Zimri peace, who slew his master? And he lifted up his face to the window, and said, 'Who is on my side?' Who? And there looked out to him two or three eunuchs. And he said, 'Throw her down.' So they threw her down and some of her blood was sprinkled on the wall, and on the horses: and he trode her under foot. And when he was come in, he did eat and drink, and said, 'Go, see now this <u>cursed woman,</u> and bury her: for she is a king's daughter.'" (2 Kings 9:30-34)

In my book "*Jezebel, Seducing Goddess of War*" we write about one of the most wicked spirits in the world today. Thousands of people have been chained by this devil. This is a controlling, manipulating, seducing, power hungry spirit that makes spiritual eunuchs out of her followers. Following this spirit can get you killed.

Eunuchs are the spiritual children of Jezebel, oftentimes referring to her as their spiritual mother. Once I gave a ministry assignment to a young man whom I was mentoring in ministry. He told me that he needed permission from his spiritual mother (someone in another city) before he could do what I asked. In a separate incident, a woman told me she had to check with an apostle (of another church) for permission to do what I asked her, even though she was no longer a member of that church. I recognized both of these people as Jezebel's eunuchs and removed them from any leadership training. When you are part of a local church that set-man is your leader, if not then you need to leave. The Holy Spirit is saying it's time to bury that cursed spirit of Jezebel.

6. THE ARROGANT AND PROUD

"Thou hast rebuked the proud that are cursed, which do err from thy commandments." (Psalms 119:21)

Not everyone that starts out with Christ ends the race with Christ. Some err and lose their way. There are many arrogant secular humanists in this world that refuse to acknowledge the lordship of Christ. Some of these were once leaders of Christian churches, others not. Just like Pharaoh they say in their hearts, "Who is the Lord that I should obey his voice?"

The arrogant and proud think more highly of themselves than they should. They feel themselves greater and above others. They are uppity and puffed up. These are the Utopians that find salvation in intellectual enlightenment and endowed to build the perfect world outside of Christ's rule. It was Sir Thomas More that first coined the term "Utopian society" in 1516. His book "Utopia" was based largely on "Plato's Republic." In the essay More describes a fictional island community in the Atlantic Ocean. It was a perfect version of society where all evils such as poverty, misery and social injustice were banished. This is nothing more than a fairy tale. Scripture is clear, "Every perfect gift comes down from above." There can be no Utopian society built by man without the Prince of Peace.

A Brother from Bangalore wrote that deliverance from all curses is available. I agree.

"Some of God's people tolerate curses instead of exposing them. The Bereans searched the Scriptures daily for understanding and truth to protect themselves from deception. People reproduce after their own kind, the unrepentant produce after the First Adam spiritual death, deception, and independence from God. Others reproduce after the Second Adam, abundant life and good works through dependence on Christ and the ministry of the Holy Spirit. Deliverance from all curses and their consequences is available through Christ's work on Calvary through true repentance and renouncement of sin."

These six curses hit their targets because of sin. They can be broken through godly sorrow, repentance, and faithful application of the blood of Jesus on your heart. There are other curses passed down the family tree because of sexual sins such as adultery, fornication, homosexuality and lesbianism. Let's take a look in the next chapter.

Chapter 4

SIX ATTACKING CURSES

Blessings are part of the Christian life and faith. Blessings are also part of the culture of the kingdom of God. People like the idea of blessings but seldom consider the consequences of sin. The Bible lets us know that the wages of sin is death. It also tells us that a man reaps what he sows. Scripture says, "The curse causeless shall not come." Yet curses with a cause will. Here are six curses looking for a cause.

1. TRUSTING IN MAN

"Thus saith the Lord; Cursed be the man that trusteth in man, and maketh flesh his arm, and whose heart departeth from the Lord. For he shall be like the heath (shrub) in the desert, and shall not see when good cometh; but shall inhabit the parched places in the wilderness, in a salt land and not inhabited." (Jeremiah 17:5-6)

Jehovah is a jealous God (Exodus 20:5). Oprah Winfrey claimed this verse turned her away from Christianity. She is host of the highest-rated talk show in television history as seen by 15 million viewers daily in 132 countries. Winfrey started her own New Age church because she believes in a mystical New Age god calling it a force. She said, "...the force, I call it God." Trusting in the spiritual self is nothing more than a perverted form of religious humanism cloaked in spiritualism. Oprah often weaves bible verses in her teachings but clearly holds to a misdirected view of God. If God does not direct a person through His Word then the only thing left are humanistic inner voices, twisted antinomian mysticism, or familiar spirits to provide guidance.

On one program with new age authors Betty Eadie,

Sophy Burnham, and Dannion Brinkley, Winfrey alluded to the book "*Ishmael*" by Daniel Quinn, saying, "One of the biggest mistakes humans make is to believe that there is only one way. Actually, there are many diverse paths leading to what you call God." A Christian in the audience corrected her saying that Jesus was the only way to God. The panel was upset to say the least. Oprah responded, "There couldn't possibly be only one way. Does God care about your heart or whether you called His Son Jesus?" The point is that man can't save himself, he needs a savior. Only Christ can fill that role. He is King of kings and Lord of lords. Scripture confirms that Oprah is wrong,

"Neither is there salvation in any other: for there is no other name under heaven given among men whereby we must be saved" (Acts 4:12).

2. FALSE MINISTERS NOT CALLED BY GOD

"Cursed be he that doeth the work of the Lord deceitfully..." (Jeremiah 48:10)

Not every minister of the Gospel is called and approved by God. Some have departed from the faith teaching deceitful doctrines of devils (1 Timothy 4:1). One young man told me of a network of these Janus-faced preachers. He wanted to repent and renounce his involvement. He said the purpose of their conferences was only for raising money, not for advancing the ministry of Christ. After services they divide the offerings among themselves. These ministers are cursed with a curse. Avoid their gospel show and performances at all cost. Don't go to their meetings or send them any money. The Holy Ghost is not with them.

3. GIVING CORRUPT OFFERINGS TO THE LORD

"Cursed be the deceiver which hath in his flock a male, and voweth, and sacrifices unto the Lord a corrupt thing: for I am a great King, saith the Lord of hosts, and my name is dreadful among the heathen." (Malachi 1:14)

You don't give to the Lord sullied offerings. One time a man knocked on the church office door. He said, "Pastor, I am on my way to the dump with these items on my truck. Come out to the parking lot and see if there is anything you might want?" I replied, "Sir, what makes you think God would want anything you are taking to the trash?"

4. NOT GIVING GOD ALL THE GLORY

"And now, O ye priests, this commandment is for you. If ye will not hear, and if ye will not lay it to heart, to give glory unto my name, saith the Lord of hosts, I will even send a curse upon you, and I will curse your blessings: yea, I have cursed them already, because ye do not lay it to heart." (Malachi 2:1-2)

One that believes prosperity and success was because of his own intelligence or brilliance will face plenty of spiritual adversity. Jesus said apart from me you can do nothing. Another verse cautions us not to think to highly of ourselves or to forget our source of blessings.

"When thou hast eaten and art full, then thou shalt bless the Lord thy God for the good land which he hath given thee. Beware that thou forget not the Lord thy God, in not keeping his commandments, and his judgments, and his statutes, which I command thee this day: Lest when thou hast eaten and art full, and hast built goodly houses, and dwelt therein; And when thy herds and thy flocks multiply, and thy silver and thy gold is multiplied, and all that thou hast is multiplied; Then thine heart be lifted up, and thou forget the Lord thy God, which brought thee forth out of the land of Egypt, from the house of bondage" (Deuteronomy 8:10-14).

5. NOT TITHING

"Will a man rob God? Yet ye have robbed me. But ye say, Wherein have we robbed thee? In tithes and offerings. Ye are cursed with a curse: for ye have robbed me, even this whole nation. Bring ye all the tithes into the storehouse, that there may be meat in mine house, and prove me now herewith, saith the Lord of hosts, if I will not open you the windows of heaven, and pour you out a blessing, that there shall not be room enough to receive it." (Malachi 3:8-10)

Jehovah was concerned for His covenant people. They were cursed with a curse. The tithe is described in Leviticus 27:30-33. A tenth of all produce or production is claimed by God as His due and is holy or set apart for Him. Christ did not repeal tithing nor did he condemn the Pharisees for tithing: "these ought ye to have done, and not to leave the other undone," meaning, "the weightier matters of the law, judgment (justice), mercy, and faith" (Matthew 23:23). To pay tithes demonstrates your oath of allegiance to Jehovah that owns all the cattle on a thousand hills. The earth is the Lords and the fullness thereof. The Holy Spirit told me that "tithing is for believers." That's a simple yet profound statement. Jehovah was clear that this curse could be broken by returning to Him with tithes and offerings. Obedience to tithing not only broke the curse but came with blessing. He promised to rebuke the devourer for their sakes and open the windows of heaven.

6. SEXUAL SINS

"Because that, when they knew God, they glorified him not as God, neither were thankful; but became vain in their imaginations, and their foolish heart was darkened. Professing themselves to be wise, they became fools, And changed the glory of the uncorruptible God into an image made like to corruptible man, and to birds, and four footed beasts, and creeping things. Wherefore God also gave them up to uncleanness through the lusts of their own hearts, to dishonor their own bodies between themselves: Who changed the truth of God into a lie, and worshiped and served the creature more than the Creator, who is blessed forever. Amen. For this cause God gave them up unto vile affections: for even their women did change the natural use into that which is against nature: And likewise also the men, leaving the natural use of the woman, burned in their lust one toward another; men with men working that which is unseemly, and receiving in themselves that recompense of their error which was meet. And even as they did not like to retain God in their knowledge, God gave them over to a reprobate mind, to do those things which are not convenient; Being filled with all unrighteousness, fornication, wickedness, covetousness, maliciousness; full of envy, murder, debate, deceit, malignity; whisperers, Backbiters, haters of God, despiteful, proud, boasters, inventors of evil things, disobedient to parents, Without understanding, covenant breakers, without natural affection, implacable (impossible to please), unmerciful: Who knowing the judgment of God, that they which commit such things are worthy of death, not only do the same, but have pleasure in them that do them." (Romans 1:21-32)

Sexual sins such as adultery, fornication, homosexuality, and lesbianism leads to destruction. As one practices these things God gives them over to uncleanness and reprobate minds. The nexus of all these sins is separation from God and doorways for generational curses.

Curses look for a cause. As already said, "The curse causeless shall not come" (Proverbs 26:2). Family curses are the result of sin or someone in the family rebelling against God. Rebellion discharges curses down the family tree. The good news is every curse can be broken through prayer, repentance, and the atoning blood of Christ.

One can come under control and bondage through spiritual witchcraft. In the next chapter we will discover how to avoid the curse of witchcraft.

Chapter 5

SPIRITUAL
WITCHCRAFT

C urses can release witchcraft within the family.
Spiritual witchcraft is the force of the enemy. The
prophet Samuel warned Saul that rebellion is as the
sin of witchcraft. Let's review how spiritual witchcraft
curses attack.

When the Spirit of the Lord departed from Saul
he spiraled slowly out of control. We watch him be
overcome by jealousy, fear, murder, divination and

finally, full blown spiritualism – which resulted in his eventual suicide.

During this period, David slew Goliath, entered the service of King Saul and eventually led one of his armies. Unknown to King Saul, God sent the Prophet Samuel to David's house when he was just a youngster to anoint him for a future day when he would replace Saul as king.

One day David and King Saul were returning from battling with the Philistines and a simple song sparked a murdering spirit of jealousy in King Saul's heart. Let's take a look.

> "And it came to pass as they came, when David was returned from the slaughter of the Philistine, that the women came out of all cities of Israel, singing and dancing, to meet King Saul, with tabrets, with joy, and with instruments of music. And the women answered one another as they played, and said, Saul hath slain his thousands, and David his ten thousands. And Saul was very wroth, and the saying displeased him; and he said, they have ascribed unto David ten thousands, and to me they have ascribed but thousands: and what can he have more but the kingdom? And

Saul eyed David from that day and forward"
(1 Samuel 18:6-9).

The pattern of destruction begins to unfold. Saul
was extremely jealous of David's anointing and the
adoration he received from the people.

Like jealous Saul, some get incensed when others
are more popular and get extra attention. When we are
walking with God, we can rest in the "peace that passes
all understanding" from such assignments against our
imaginations (Philippians 4:7). When we step out
of peace through rebellion, then fear, jealousy and
insecurity rule our life. Fear always releases insecurity
and causes one to be very controlling.

Remember, too, that witchcraft desires to control
the environment around it. Anyone who threatens that
environment is viewed as a danger. This is how Saul
viewed David – a threat to his ministry. To manage that
threat, Saul became controlling and was overcome by
a murderous spirit.

DIVINATION
THROUGH PROPHECY

Witchcraft continued to impose a serious levy on Saul
as he stepped into the realm of false prophecy. David

was at King Saul's house to witness him prophesying by a spirit of divination. Scripture says,

> "And it came to pass on the morrow, that the evil spirit from God came upon Saul, and he prophesied in the midst of the house: and David played with his hand, as at other times: and there was a javelin in Saul's hand" (1 Samuel 18:10).

Did Saul prophesy? Yes, but by what spirit was he prophesying? It was a spirit of divination.

Scripture clearly states that the Spirit of the Lord departed from Saul, yet we watch him prophesy. His prophetic utterance, however, was not given to him by the Holy Spirit, but, rather, by an evil spirit. This is why all prophecy must be judged. For every true gifting of God there is a counterfeit. We must be capable of discerning what spirit is at work and allow all prophetic utterances to be examined carefully (1 Thessalonians 5:21). This is the judgment of mature ministry gifts. Let's not be afraid to judge all prophetic utterances. Only those operating through witchcraft would disagree.

A MURDEROUS SPIRIT

When King Saul finishes prophesying, he throws the javelin that was in his hand at David. David was completely innocent. He had no idea that the anointing on his life was causing this murdering spirit to manifest. Scripture says,

> "And the evil spirit from the Lord was upon Saul, as he sat in his house with his javelin in his hand: and David played with his hand. And Saul sought to smite David even to the wall with the javelin; but he slipped away out of Saul's presence, and he smote the javelin into the wall: and David fled, and escaped that night" (1 Samuel 19:9-10).

Saul attempted to murder David because of jealousy. Witchcraft hates the voice and the anointing of God. David had no choice but to flee from a man he truly loved to save his own life. Saul, representative of one with a religious spirit (religion is a murdering spirit), attempts to murder David, an innocent young man who loves God.

Moreover, Saul pursued David to Nob, the city of priest, and in his murderous rage orders Doeg to kill forty-five of God's priests to get information regarding David's whereabouts.

Witchcraft will murder anybody it views as a threat to its kingdom (ministry). Scripture says,

> "And the king said to Doeg, turn thou, and fall upon the priests. And Doeg the Edomite turned, and he fell upon the priests, and slew on that day fourscore and five persons that did wear a linen ephod. And Nob, the city of the priests, smote he with the edge of the sword, men and women, children and sucklings, and oxen, and asses, and sheep, with the edge of the sword" (1 Samuel 22:18-19).

FULL-BLOWN SPIRITUALISM

Saul attempts to pray, but again, God refuses to answer him.

> "And when Saul inquired of the Lord, the Lord answered him not, neither by dreams, nor by Urim, nor by prophets. Then said Saul unto his servants, seek me a woman that hath a familiar spirit that I may go to her, and inquire of her. And his servants said to him, Behold, there is a woman that hath a familiar spirit

at Endor. And Saul disguised himself, and put on other raiment, and he went, and two men with him, and they came to the woman by night: and he said, I pray thee, divine unto me by the familiar spirit, and bring me him up, whom I shall name unto thee" (1 Samuel 28:6-8).

Saul frantically inquired of God, yet God's voice had left him. What Saul didn't realize was that true repentance is the criteria for God's ear.

Notice, too, that Saul sought prophetic dreams. In his desperation for a prophetic word, he entered into full-blown spiritualism by seeking out the witch of Endor. God strictly forbade seeking the prophetic services from one with a familiar spirit. How many today allow the spirit of witchcraft to encourage them to ignore God's Word and attempt to gain spiritual insight illegally through familiar spirits? Such attempts release curses down the family linage.

> The end result of witchcraft and spiritualism is death.

While preaching in Holland, I read a newspaper report that half of the population of Italy was seeking out spiritualists to prophesy their futures. The most shocking thing, however, was that eighty percent of the seekers were "church" people. Deception is never prejudiced.

THE SWORD

> "Then said Saul unto his armorbearer, Draw thy sword, and thrust me through therewith; lest these uncircumcised come and thrust me through, and abuse me. But his armorbearer would not; for he was sore afraid. Therefore Saul took a sword, and fell upon it" (1 Samuel 31:4).

From these scriptures we see the gradual decline and fall of a man once anointed by God to be king. At the very root of the deception was spiritual pride, wanting to be seen of men and fearing them more than God.

The end result of witchcraft and spiritualism is death. Scripture declares,

> "So Saul died for his transgression which he committed against the Lord, even against the word of the Lord, which he kept not, and also for asking counsel of one that had a familiar spirit, to inquire of it; And inquired not of

the Lord: therefore he slew him, and turned the kingdom unto David the son of Jesse" (1 Chronicles 10:13-14).

QUESTIONS

Examine your heart by asking yourself these questions:

Do you feel drawn to super spiritual activity?

Are you seeking prophecy, dreams and visions?

Do you run after every new revelation?

Are you jealous of someone else's gifting?

Do you feel that others should recognize your gifting and does it really bother you when they don't?

Do you have a tendency to follow spiritual experiences without first undertaking a careful examination of the Word of God?

Do you think you are more spiritual than others?

Do you have a tendency to change your opinion of scripture based on whom you're talking to at the time?

Is anyone you know feeding your spiritual pride?

Are you obedient to do the commandments of God in your life?

Are you seeking diplomas, awards and trophies so as to be seen by man?

Do you crave positive public opinion?

Are you always blaming others for your problems?

Are you looking for the recognition and honor of men?

Do you judge all personal prophecies?

Are you reading the horoscope, calling psychics and seeking for personal prophesies?

Are you climbing a religious ladder?

Has anyone in your family done these thing?

WITCHCRAFT'S CONTROL

Control is a form of witchcraft. The Apostle Paul wrote,

> "Now the Lord is that Spirit: and where the Spirit of the Lord is, there is liberty" (2 Corinthians 3:17).

Witchcraft is clearly seen by the actions of controlling people. Once witchcraft (operating through a person) has controlled you, it doesn't want to let go. Even when the person lives in another city they are constantly reaching back into the lives of those they once controlled. You find yourself getting that unexpected phone call with the words, "God just keeps putting you on my heart."

Controllers will try to harass a person for years. They are so persistent that you can seldom offend them. The yoke of witchcraft, however, must be broken through prayer and, yes, even direct confrontation, if necessary. Like Saul's relationship with David, if witchcraft can't control you it will attempt to murder you. Today, witchcraft murders people with slanderous words and false accusations. I wrote much on this subject in my book *"Exposing Spiritual Witchcraft."*

Controllers quiz you extensively to find out everything they can about your life and they tell you very little about themselves. Hidden things and secrecy are part of the witchcraft agenda. You can sense that their phone conversations are usually one-sided. They will spend as much time as you will let them in *probing* conversation about your problems – but watch out for their false motives.

People operating in witchcraft will flatter you to your face, but stab you in the back. Many times these spirits will tell you what they think you want to hear so you won't leave their controlling influence. They have fake anointings and are dominant in nature. The motives of manipulation are to obtain control and status. They are deceitful servants with wrong motives. They serve with a "what's-in-it-for-me" attitude.

Witchcraft wants to advance its selfish cause at any price. When you refuse to submit to it, only then will it have no further use of you. It will discard you and begin looking for its next victim. Beware of its final murderous attack because witchcraft likes to kill what it can't control.

WRAPPED IN DECEPTION

The spirit of witchcraft must be held accountable. You cannot submit to controlling spirits. Those under the influence of witchcraft, like Saul, never think they are doing anything wrong. I have heard people who were caught in blatant sin tell me that they did nothing wrong and have nothing to feel sorry about. They get so wrapped up in deception that they will not allow the Spirit of God to bring them to repentance. When caught, they act like innocent lambs.

Like Saul, those deceived by witchcraft get lifted up in pride. They think they are the ones that "make the world go around."

Listen to them talk. They will flatter you with gifts and kiss up to you; yet, there is always some kind of string attached. When someone flatters you, listen to your heart. If you sense a check (red light) in your spirit – beware. Never violate the inner witness in your spirit. That red light is God's Spirit cautioning you. In the last days, witchcraft spirits will attempt to control the liberty of the Spirit Himself and kill the prophetic voice of God.

LEGALISTIC

Witchcraft is legalistic and looks for assistants.

More specifically, a person operating in the spirit of witchcraft is legalistic when it comes to you, but does not hold themselves to the same letter of the law. This evil spirit will use you until it perceives that you are a threat to its supposed arena of authority or that you serve no further purpose. Witchcraft controllers are always looking for assistants, vessels to carry and guard their manipulations.

Beware! Watch for controllers who try to manipulate and dominate you and your time, with all sorts of witchcraft and words of intimidation.

QUESTIONS

Examine your heart by asking yourself these questions:

Do you fear public opinion more than God's opinion?

Is someone intentionally hindering your spiritual maturity?

Is there someone from your past who continues to try and control you?

Is there someone telling you what they think you want to hear?

Has anyone given you a gift with strings attached?

Have you ever felt used?

WITCHCRAFT AND THE SPIRIT OF JEZEBEL

The spirit of Jezebel operates in witchcraft. Jezebel is a controlling manipulating spirit of witchcraft.

Witchcraft spirits will attack you when you hold them accountable. Jezebels say things like, "You are non-loving and mean." But true Christian love must address areas that are out of order in your life.

As we discussed previously, a religious person, who is self-centered and prideful, is a target for witchcraft curses. These folks gauge their spirituality by the length of time they pray and the amount of religious works they do. But when people are operating in the spirit of Jezebel, they are not putting anything into the relationship, but are only using you to advance their selfish motivations. When witchcraft is released at you it makes you feel used.

People operating in the spirit of Jezebel (controlling witchcraft) seldom repent of their harmful actions and can be very brazen and outwardly aggressive to cover up their insecurities. Even when wrong, they will not admit to their improprieties. Instead, they talk about being "broken and poured out" but only as a camouflage to hide their sinister motives. Insecurity puts on a bold facade as a protection so as not to be rejected.

The Jezebel spirit will size you up and do whatever it takes to find your weakness. Whatever you're susceptible to, it will attack you in that area. To learn more about the spirit of Jezebel, check out my book *"Jezebel: Seducing Goddess of War."*

Are their things in you house that curses can attach themselves to? Find out how to do a spiritual house cleaning in the next chapter.

Chapter 6

BREAKING
WORD CURSES

Family curses can be identified. They are familiar problems that continue to reoccur within the family tree. Scripture says that God visits the iniquity of the fathers upon the children up to the third and fourth generation (Exodus 20:5). Curses don't visit your family without a cause. Sometimes spiritual weapons formed against you are the result of word curses. The good news is all word curses can be broken.

Are you a victim of word curses? Violent crimes include homicide, rape, robbery, and assault. Property crimes include burglary, theft, motor vehicle theft and arson. We are familiar with these types of crimes but what about crimes committed by word curses? You have probably heard this children's idiom, "Sticks and stones can break my bones but words can never hurt me." Don't you wish that were true? It's not. Words are powerful and they can hurt. Words are not neutral, they can release blessing or cursing.

> Words can be creative or destructive, encourage or condemn, bless or curse.

Words spoken from strangers and those with authority are different. A father, for example, can bless or curse. The weight of the father's place of governing authority has great influence in the realm of the spirit. The words of a parent can have a lasting impact on children both good and bad.

Scripture declares life and death are in the power of the tongue (Proverbs 28:21). Words can be creative or destructive, encourage or condemn, bless or curse. The words bless, blessed and blessing are found in 468 verses in the King James Bible and curse, cursed, and cursing 172.

When God created the earth He blessed it. When he created Adam and Eve He blessed them. Abraham was blessed. Scripture declares,

"And I will make of thee a great nation, and I will bless thee, and make thy name great; and thou shalt be a blessing. And I will bless them that bless thee, and curse him that curseth thee: and in thee shall all families of the earth be blessed." (Genesis 12:2-3).

Jesus spoke of blessing,

"Blessed are the poor in spirit: for theirs is the kingdom of heaven. Blessed are they that mourn: for they shall be comforted. Blessed are the meek: for they shall inherit the earth. Blessed are they which do hunger and thirst after righteousness: for they shall be filled. Blessed are the merciful: for they shall obtain mercy. Blessed are the pure in heart: for they shall see God. Blessed are the peacemakers: for they shall be called the children of God. Blessed are they which are persecuted for righteousness' sake: for theirs is the kingdom of heaven. Blessed are ye, when men shall revile you, and persecute you, and shall say all

manner of evil against you falsely, for my sake."
(Matthew 5:3-11)

Blessings are part of the Christian life and faith. Blessings are also part of the culture of the kingdom of God. People like the idea of passing blessings down the family tree but seldom consider the possibility of passing curses down the family tree. When speaking of curses we are not talking about releasing demonic spirits through voodoo, magic spells, or ceremonial witchcraft prayers but simply using the power of words. A curse can be any expressed wish that some form of adversity or misfortune would come upon someone.

When word curses are released demon spirits attach themselves to those curses ever eager to perform harm and hurt. These are destroying spirits. As already said words can bless or hurt, wound, and scar. This is why gossip and backbiting is forbidden. Thousands need inner healing because of word curses. Time heals wounds but scars remain. The good news is Christ your healer. As it is written, "By His stripes you were healed." Healing and deliverance was provided in the atoning blood of Jesus both emotional and physical.

Those in authority carry much weight in the spirit. They can be parents, teachers, employers, church leaders, or those one admires. When a person in authority tells a child they are no good, ugly, fat, will amount to nothing, will never make it, and if that child believes what he or she hears then seeds of condemnation are planted. Scripture says, "As a man thinketh in his heart so is he." Seeds come up. Some crops come in sooner than later. In my book "_Life After Rejection: God's path to emotional healing_" we talk about receiving inner healing from hurts still buried alive in people.

> Devils don't play fair. They don't care what you meant to say, they respond to what you said.

A man told me when he was a little boy his father repeatedly released word curses over him saying things like, "You will never accomplish anything." Throughout his life when taking exams or trying to complete projects he would have lots of trouble. Even though he would approach exams and undertakings in faith and enthusiasm he would still have trouble getting through the materials and finishing tasks. After hearing about family curses he renounced the iniquities up his family tree, broke all the word curses spoken over his life, forgave his father, and received Christ' deliverance from curses. The results manifested. Those unseen spiritual hindrances completing exams and task were gone.

GENERATION TO GENERATION

Family curses get passed from generation to generation. Many pass down through words. It is heart breaking to hear a parent repeat to their children the same words that hurt them. This is why parents should be careful what they speak over their children.

The Apostle James taught,

> "The tongue can no man tame; it is an unruly evil, full of deadly poison. Therewith bless we God, even the Father; and therewith curse we men, which are made after the similitude of God. Out of the same mouth proceedeth blessing and cursing. My brethren, these things ought not so to be" (James 3:8-10).

Word curses can be discovered in many common sayings. Here are a few simple examples:

1. You will never amount to anything.
2. You are just like your father, good for nothing.
3. You are the dumbest kid in the world.
4. You get sick the same time every year.
5. We never had anything and you won't either.
6. Everybody in the family has been divorced and you're marriage won't last either.

7. Everybody in the family has died young and you will too.
8. This family is always getting into trouble with the law.
9. Daddy was a drunk and you will be too.
10. This drives me crazy.
11. Whenever there is a flu bug I catch it.
12. I don't think I will ever get pregnant.
13. I can't afford to tithe.
14. I can never make ends meet.
15. Over my dead body.
16. I'm sick and tired.
17. This always happens to me.
18. Every year about this time I catch a cold.
19. I'm just accident prone.
20. I just can't get up on time.

Devils don't play fair. They don't care what you meant to say, they respond to what you said. Remembering this will help you overcome. It is written that you overcome by the blood of the Lamb and the word of your testimony. Let your testimony be words of life over yourself and others. Jesus said, "Bless and curse not." Walking in God's blessings is a choice. Use your tongue choosing to bless and not curse.

Family curses can pass down the family tree through word curses. Those curses can be identified when certain iniquities manifest within the family linage. As already said sometimes spiritual weapons formed against you are the result of word curses. The good news is all word curses can be broken.

Freedom has already been provided by Christ. Deliverance belongs to you. Scripture says, "No weapon formed against you shall prosper and every tongue that rises against you in judgment you shall condemn." Deliverance from word curses belongs to you. It is part of "the heritage of the servants of the Lord" (Isaiah 54:17).

Are there things in your house that curses can attach themselves to? Find out how to do a spiritual house cleaning in the next chapter.

Chapter 7

SPIRITUAL HOUSE CLEANING

M ature believers don't let the demons of family members past alter their futures. Scripture says that God visits the iniquity of the fathers upon the children unto the third and fourth generation. These visits of iniquity are called family curses. Demon powers and familiar spirits look for generational curses.

Family curses are broken through identification, repentance, forgiveness, and spiritual house cleanings.

Family curses don't come without a cause (Proverbs 26:2). The cause can be sin, demonic covenants and agreements, or iniquities coming down the family tree. In other words someone in your family tree could be the reason for unholy demonic visitations. The good news is that Christ has already paid the price and deliverance provided by His atoning blood (Galatians 3:13). After family curses have been discovered and broken it's a good idea to do a spiritual house cleaning.

> Spirits can come and go as they please in your home if they consider your home their home.

Spirits can come and go as they please in your home if they consider your home their home. No demons however can enter or stay in your home without legal grounds. Those legal grounds are sometimes family curses. Squatters have no legal grounds to settle on property. They are illegal's and can be evicted by court order. Family curses are the same. They too can be evicted when heaven's court orders are served. Once family curses are broken demon spirits must flee. The only thing that can give them legal rights to stick around your house is having their property.

CASTLE DOCTRINE

Scripture says, "Through wisdom a house is built and by understanding it is established" (Proverbs 24:3). Your home is your castle. The "Castle Doctrine" came from English Common Law designating one's place of residence as a place to enjoy protection from illegal trespassing and violent attacks.

The Bible commentator Matthew Henry wrote,

"A man's house is his castle and God's law, as well as man's, sets a guard upon it; he that assaults it does so at his peril." And the Roman philosopher Marcus Cicero wrote, "What more sacred, what more strongly guarded by every holy feeling, than a man's own home?"

A man's house is his castle. It is your place of spiritual jurisdiction. As both a priest and king you have been authorized as head of your house. You are in charge. What you bind on earth is bound in heaven and what you loose on earth is loosed in heaven. That gives you spiritual authority to open and close doors. It gives you the authorization to forbid demon powers from entering or staying. It also means what you allow in your house God allows, what you forbid in your house God forbids. Scripture declares, "The wicked are overthrown and are not but the house of the righteous shall stand" (Proverbs 12:7).

Mature believers understand spiritual warfare and deliverance. Spiritual warfare is simply binding and loosing in prayer and attacking on purpose spiritual strongholds of opposition and resistance against the gospel of Christ in your life (Matthew 18:18-20). It is taking up, in prayer, the authority of the believer that Jesus gave His disciples (Luke 10:17).

Satan understands spiritual warfare and deliverance. He uses man's sins, family curses, and scriptural ignorance of delegated spiritual authority to attack him and enter his home. This is why it is important to renew your mind with the Word of God (Romans 12:1-3). Satan has no authority over you unless you remain in sin or stay ignorant of his tactics. Scripture says, Submit yourself to God, resist the devil and he shall flee" (James 1:8). It is you that must do the resisting.

THESE MUST GO

You can't love out, counsel out, or drug out demon spirits. They must be cast out. After you receive forgiveness of all family sins and iniquities do a spiritual house cleaning. A spiritual house cleaning involves removing all demonic:

- Books
- Games
- Videos
- Photos
- Paintings
- Artifacts
- Music
- Statues
- Jewelry
- Candles

Don't give the devil any place within your home. Demonic items give spirits legal rights to remain in your home. You can't cast them out if you don't throw their property out too.

Those that believed the preaching of the Apostle Paul were convicted of sin, repented, and brought their demonic books and burned them. They did a spiritual house cleaning. Scripture says, "And many that believed came, and confessed, and showed their deeds. Many of them also which used curious arts brought their books together, and burned them before all men: and they counted the price of them, and found it fifty thousand pieces of silver" (Acts 19:18-19). Today fifty thousand pieces of silver is over a million dollars.

Some pray Psalm 91, others the Lord's Prayer, throughout their homes while anointing all entries with oil. The how-too will vary. Ask the Holy Spirit to lead and guide you. He will.

As already said some do a prayer walk through their homes. They do that by walking from room to room blessing each room and occupant, and binding any demon spirits that might be trying to stay. They then pray for every family member's bedroom and every entrance to the home. It's a good idea to have all your believing family members pray with you. If one can put a thousand to flight then two can put ten thousand.

As a citizen of the kingdom of God you have spiritual authority over your home and possessions. When you pray do so with authority remembering that greater is He that is in you than he that is in the world. Christ gave you power over serpents, scorpions, and over all the power of the enemy and nothing by any means shall harm you.

As you go from room to room pray Christ's blessings of peace declaring "Thy Kingdom come thy will be done on earth just as it is in heaven." While walking throughout your home, invite the Holy Spirit to dwell in each habitation commanding the powers of darkness to leave in Jesus Name. You can also apply anointing oil on each door throughout the house decreeing God's holiness and purpose for your family's life. Finally ask the Lord to assign His angels to watch over your family and property, and for His blood covenant protection.

Now that you have broken all family curses, cleared your home of demonic items, and blessed your castle, use your faith and receive Christ's blessings for your entire household. Scripture says, "What things soever ye desire, when ye pray, believe that ye receive them, and ye shall have them" (Mark 11:24).

There are important but quick and easy steps toward deliverance from family curses. In the following chapter learn how to walk them out.

Chapter 8

DELIVERANCE FROM FAMILY CURSES

You can experience deliverance from a family curse. A study of family curses brings to light information in areas people don't talk much about. When topics like this are addressed it demystifies feelings that you are the only one experiencing such feelings. Understanding family curses takes the mystery away and helps you find the road to freedom.

I've got good news for you. It's a new day. Deliverance from family curses has already been provided. You don't have to wait any more. Understanding what belongs to you is a key in stopping family curses. Christ has already paid the price for iniquity and provided deliverance through his sacrifice on Calvary.

Just like every promise in Scripture you must receive it by faith. That also includes deliverance from family curses. We know that faith cometh by hearing and hearing by the Word of God (Romans 10:17). In other words, you need to know what belongs to you as a son or daughter of the Father first then you can pray, believe, receive, and take action. Knowledge plus faith leads toward freedom.

Christ has already redeemed you from the curse of the law of sin and death. Redemption means the price for sin has already been paid. The curse of the law is the recompense for iniquity. Recompense includes the rightful payment for iniquities from sin in your family tree. A family tree is a chart representing family relationships in a conventional tree structure. Scripture confirms this truth,

> "Christ hath redeemed us from the curse of the law being made a curse for us: For it is written cursed is every one that hangeth on a tree" (Galatians 3:13).

A Sister from Kerala, India writes that knowledge of the Word of God helped her get free from family curses.

"The Word of God helps people free themselves from family curses that follow them without their knowledge. A few years ago, before I realized what was happening to our family, we were experiencing all kinds of sorrows and pains. These were coming from a family curse. The Holy Spirit gave me the revelation to submit to God, resist the devil, and use my faith to fight back in the mighty name of Jesus. I started decreeing that we were God's children and family curses had no authority or power over us."

A mother living in North Carolina discovered why she and family suffered from addictions and marriage problems.

"Our family line has been under curses of addiction, poverty mentality, men in prison, men that committed murder, women having kids out of wedlock, and women not marrying. The Lord delivered me from alcohol and a life of ignorance and poverty. I have seen family curses trailing my family as we came through many fiery trials with our children. I was able to trace certain strongholds in my own life and learned why I responded to situations the way I did. Many of these were unbroken family curses."

A woman in Georgia was concerned that occult spirits were waging war against her because of a family curse.

"My father was a 33rd Degree Mason and mother part of the Eastern Star. They both renounced their involvement before passing away. The information about family curses helped me break them. Knowledge of these types of curses needs to be taught in the Church. Many believers don't know the effects of generational curses on their families and the importance of breaking them. I was one of them until I gained knowledge of this teaching. After breaking the family curses over my life and children I noticed a change when praying. I did not have to war in the spirit as much. The spiritual resistance when praying was gone. I repented for the iniquity of my father, mother, and past leaders in my family. My husband and I shared this insight with our children too. We don't want any generational curses attacking them."

Scripture declares, Jesus "bruised" on the cross for the penalty of family iniquities.

"Surely he hath borne our griefs and carried our sorrows: yet we did esteem him stricken, smitten of God, and afflicted. But he was wounded for our transgressions; he was bruised for our iniquities: the chastisement of our peace was upon him; and with his stripes we are healed. All we like sheep have gone astray; we have turned every one to his own way; and the Lord hath laid on him the iniquity of us all" (Isaiah 53:4-6).

The crucifixion —death, burial, and resurrection of the Lord is great news. Now all you have to do is receive what Christ has already provided, deliverance from every family curse. Scripture says,

"And it shall come to pass that whosoever shall call on the name of the Lord shall be delivered: for in mount Zion and in Jerusalem shall be deliverance, as the Lord hath said, and in the remnant whom the Lord shall call" (Joel 2:32).

The right to call on the name of the Lord for deliverance from family curses belongs to you. Don't let anything hold you back. Call on His name right now.

Here is part of the biblical pattern for breaking family curses:

Confess all known and unknown sins both personal and up the family tree.

"For with the heart man believeth unto righteousness; and with the mouth confession is made unto salvation." (Romans 10:10)

Repent of rebellion and unforgiveness.

"For godly sorrow worketh repentance to salvation not to be repented of: but the sorrow of the world worketh death." (2 Corinthians 7:10)

Godly sorrow is a deep heart-felt repentance that leads to deliverance.

"And when ye stand praying, forgive, if ye have ought against any: that your Father also which is in heaven may forgive you your trespasses. But if ye do not forgive, neither will your Father

which is in heaven forgive your trespasses."
(Mark 11:24-26)

Confess Jesus as Lord, Savior, and Deliverer.

"The Spirit of the Lord is upon me, because
he hath anointed me to preach the gospel
to the poor; he hath sent me to heal the
brokenhearted, to preach deliverance to the
captives, and recovering of sight to the blind,
to set at liberty them that are bruised, to
preach the acceptable year of the Lord." (Luke
4:18-19) Some want Christ as savior, not lord.
Jesus said, "Why call me Lord and do not the
things I say?" (Luke 6:46)

**Renounce all contact with
the forbidden such as witchcraft, the occult,
satanic involvement, idolatry, involvement in
secret societies, and forbidden activities.**

"And many that believed came, and confessed,
and shewed their deeds. Many of them also
which used curious arts brought their books
together, and burned them before all men:
and they counted the price of them, and
found it fifty thousand pieces of silver. So

mightily grew the word of God and prevailed." (Acts 19:18-20)

Claim this promise of deliverance for yourself and family.

"If they shall confess their iniquity, and the iniquity of their fathers, with their trespass which they trespassed against me, and that also they have walked contrary unto me; And that I also have walked contrary unto them, and have brought them into the land of their enemies; if then their uncircumcised hearts be humbled, and they then accept of the punishment of their iniquity: Then will I remember my covenant with Jacob, and also my covenant with Isaac, and also my covenant with Abraham will I remember; and I will remember the land" (Leviticus 26:40).

"There is therefore now no condemnation to those who are in Christ Jesus, who do not walk according to the flesh, but according to the Spirit" (Romans 8:1).

This is key when breaking family curses. As you walk in the Spirit, doing what's pleasing to the Holy Spirit, curses lose their control over your destiny. As a child of God you are no longer a servant to sin. Whom the Son sets free is free indeed.

Get in agreement with this Scripture.

"If we confess our sins, he is faithful and just to forgive us our sins, and to cleanse us from all unrighteousness" (1 John 1:9).

So after you have confessed, repented, and prayed, believe this too. "What things soever ye desire, when ye pray, believe that ye receive them, and ye shall have them" (Mark 11:24).

Family curses are real. They can visit because of your sin or sins by relatives up your family tree. It is written that God visits the iniquities of the fathers upon the children to the third and fourth generation. It is comforting to know that deliverance from family curses belongs to you through the atoning blood of Christ.

PRAYER

Heavenly Father, thank You for the authority to battle against family generational curses that attack me and my household. In Jesus Name I bind every negative unscriptural word spoken against my life. I break the power of confusion, torment, fear, control and witchcraft. I take captive every vain imagination and high thing that is contrary to God's plan for my life.

I submit my will, thoughts and life to the Lordship of Christ Jesus and plead the blood of Jesus over my mind, commanding stability and order to prevail in my soul.

I break the power of every family curse of hereditary sicknesses, poverty, abuse, family problems, drug addiction, murder, witchcraft's deception, seduction, sorcery and fear, knowing that at the name of Jesus every knee must bow.

I decree freedom from generational curses, visiting sins, demon spirits, Jezebel, sexual sins, alcohol and drugs, controllers, manipulators, sorcerers, witches, counterfeits, soul ties, spiritual folly, soothsayers, lying spirits, lying dreams and visions.

I repent of the sins committed up and down my family line, both known and unknown, and submit myself thoroughly to the Lordship of Jesus Christ and His word.

I clothe myself with God's armor and take up the weapons of my warfare that are not carnal, but mighty in the pulling down of strongholds.

I dedicate myself to the will of Jesus Christ alone for my life.

I repent of rebellion, pride, arrogance, spiritualism, control, manipulation, vain desires, not being in church, and disrespecting the five-fold ascension gifts and my leaders.

I renounce every family generational curse now.

Lord, your Word says, "If I confess my sins You are faithful and just to forgive me of my sins and cleanse me of all unrighteousness."

Thank you Jesus that you said you would never leave me nor forsake me, even to the end of the age.

Amen.

FAMILY CURSES AND DELIVERANCE CHECKLIST

When breaking family curses and deliverance it may be helpful to call out certain iniquities, spirits and curses. Here is a partial list:

A

Abortion
Abuse
Accusation
Addiction
Adultery
Ahab
Alcohol
Allergies
Anger
Anxiety
Argument
Arrogance
Arthritis
Asthma
Astrology

B

Backbiting
Beelzebub
Bestiality
Bickering
Bitterness
Blasphemy
Blindness
Broken heart
Broken spirit

C

Card reading
Charms
Child abuse
Clairvoyant
Compromise

Confusion
Contention
Control
Covetousness
Criticism
Cruelty
Cultism
Cursing

D

Deaf and dumb
Death
Deception
Defeatism
Depression
Despair
Destruction
Discouragement
Disobedience
Distrust
Divination
Divorce
Dominance
Doubt
Dread
Drugs
Drunkenness

E

ESP
Envy
Error
False prophesy
False religions
Familiar spirits
Family curses
Fantasy lust
Fatigue
Faultfinding
Fear
Fear of man
Fighting
Forgetfulness
Fornication
Fortune telling
Frigidity
Frustration

G

Generational curses
Gossip
Greed
Grief

H

Harlotry
Hatred
Heaviness
Homosexuality
Hopelessness
Horoscope
Hurt

I

Idleness
Impotent
Inadequacy
Incantation
Incest
Incubus
Indecision
Indifference
Inferiority
Infirmities
Iniquities
Inner hurts
Inner pain
Insanity
Insecurity
Insomnia

J

Jealousy
Jezebel
Judging

K

Kundalini

L

Lawlessness
Laziness
Legalism
Lesbianism
Levitation
Loneliness
Love of money
Lying

M

Madness
Magic
Mania
Masturbation
Medium

Mental illness
Mind control
Mocking
Murder

N

Necromancy
Nervousness
New Age
Nightmares

O

Obesity
Occult
Oppression

P

Panics
Paranoia
Passivity
Perversion
Pornography
Possessiveness
Pouting
Prejudice

Pressure
Pride
Prostitution

Q

Quarreling
Queen of Heaven

R

Rape
Rebellion
Rejection
Resentment
Retaliation
Revenge

S

Sadism
Sadness
Schizophrenia
Secret societies
Seduction
Self-deception
Self-pity
Self-rejection

Self-righteousness
Self-will
Selfishness
Serpent power
Sexual perversion
Shame
Shyness
Sickness
Smoking
Sodomy
Soothsayer
Sorrow
Spirit of anti-Christ
Spirit of bondage
Spiritualism
Spite
Stealing
Stress
Strife
Stubbornness
Succubus
Suicide
Superstitions
Suspicion

T

Tarot Cards

Temper
Terrors
Timidity
Torment
Trance

U

Unbelief
Uncleanness
Unclean spirits
Unforgiving
Unsubmissive
Unteachable
Unworthiness

V

Vagabond
Vampirism
Violence

W

Weakness
Weariness
Whoredoms
Witchcraft

Word curses
Worldliness
Worry

Y

Yoga

INVITATION TO DESTINY

Are you hungry for more of God? In addition to preaching the Gospel around the world, we also pastor a powerful, Spirit-filled church in South Florida. The Spirit of God told us to build a church from which to send forth believers that could reach their cities and impact the nations for Jesus Christ.

Have you been searching for God only to find religion? Spirit of Life Ministries (SOLM) is a multicultural church where all races gather together in unity and cares for the needs of the whole family. Is something missing from your life? SOLM is a church where you can receive what you need from the Lord. We believe in divine healing, manifesting the gifts of the Spirit, prayer results, miracles, prosperity, finding purpose and making a difference. With God all things are possible.

Are you looking for a place to grow? SOLM is a new apostolic church with all five-fold ministry gifts operating. We have a prophetic call and mandate to equip, activate and release every believer into the work of the ministry according to Ephesians 4:11-12. We invite you to come and connect with your destiny and receive confirmation, impartation and activation for your life.

Come adventure with us,
Jonas and Rhonda Clark

SPIRIT OF LIFE MINISTRIES WORLD HEADQUARTERS
27 WEST HALLANDALE BEACH BLVD. • HALLANDALE BEACH, FLA. 33009
800.943.6490 • WWW.JONASCLARK.COM

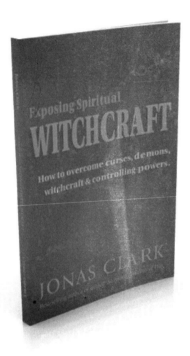

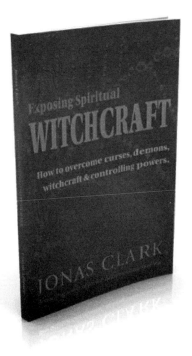

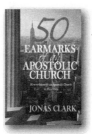
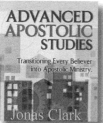
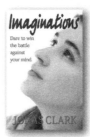

Easy Read Pocket-sized Books

Jezebel & Prophetic Ministry • Entering Prophetic Ministry
How Witchcraft Spirits Attack • Seeing What Others Can't
Unlocking Prophetic Imaginations

Healing Rejection & Emotional Abuse • Overcoming Dark Imaginations
What To Do When You Feel Like Giving Up • Prophecy Without
Permission • The Weapons of Your Warfare

More Titles: Avoiding Foreign Spirits • How Prophets Fail •
Breaking Christian Witchcraft • Identifying Prophetic Spirit-
ists • How Jezebel Hijacks Prophetic Ministry • Unlocking Your
Spiritual Authority • Prophetic Confrontation

For more easy read Pocket-sized books
visit www.JonasClark.com
or call 800.943.6490.

Jonas Clark's Revolutionary Review Newsletter

Topic: *Becoming a King in God's Kingdom*

You double opted-in to receive Jonas Clark's Revolutionary Review Newsletter. You subscribed as *webmaster@jonasclark.com*.

Jonas prays daily for his partners in Christ.

View this e-mail in your browser.

Home | Blog | Global Cause Network | Book Reviews | Bookstore

Becoming a King in God's Kingdom

By Jonas Clark

Kingship is acting on your spiritual authority to invade, occupy and influence the world around you. It is fulfilling the first great commission to "multiply, produce, increase, subdue and take dominion." Today, however, it seems everyone wants to be a prophet and no one a king. What good is a low-level prophetic word while the wicked continue to rule over God's people?

Anything dealing with prophetic ministry is hot. I have a pocket-sized book out entitled "Entering Prophetic Ministry" that people are ordering like hot cakes. In this book I write about how to enter prophetic ministry. It seems everyone wants to be a prophet. The danger

GOVERNING BELIEVERS:
Your apostolic nature is found in three words: **building, restoring and governing.**
These three ruling properties

Receive bi-weekly FREE articles from Jonas Clark to equip you for your destiny.Read present truth articles on topics such as apostolic ministry, spritual warfare, deliverance, prophetic ministry, Kingdom living and more.

Sign up today @
www.JonasClark.com

Want to learn more about becoming
effective in life and ministry?

Find answers in THE VOICE® magazine.

Sign up to receive a
FREE Issue of THE VOICE® magazine
at www.thevoicemagazine.com

Kingdom Living
Dominion, Authority, Purpose

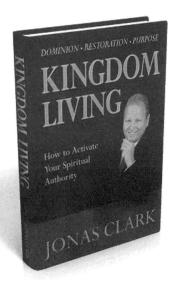

ISBN 978-1-886885-21-9
HardCover

Are you experiencing Kingdom Living?

Jonas shows you how to activate your kingship and live a life of purpose, authority and dominion that belongs to you in Christ.

Kingdom Living offers practical insights into what Jesus meant when He said, "It is the Father's good pleasure to give unto you the Kingdom."

This book unlocks mysteries of the Kingdom for your life. When you read *Kingdom Living* you will discover how to tap into the power of the Kingdom of God in you and how to pray the way Jesus prayed.

Kingdom Living equips you with action steps designed to help you experience what the Bible says about restoration, dominion, spiritual authority – and your role in the Kingdom of God.

To order Kingdom Living, call 800.943.6490 or visit www.JonasClark.com.

Effective Ministries & Believers
Introducing apostolic ministry and what it means to you.

Christ's disciples have fought raging spiritual battles with Satan for centuries. Some failed, others experienced limited success, but there is another group, effective believers that discovered the secret to victorious living. This group was taught by apostles that Christ would "build his church and the gates of hell would not prevail against it."

ISBN 978-1-886885-25-7

In ***Effective Ministries and Believers*** learn:

- Get the most out of your calling.
- Make a difference with your life.
- Discover God's design for effective ministry.
- Discover restoration and reformation principles.
- Gain spiritual strength to reach the next level.
- Learn how to invade, occupy and influence.
- And much more!

To order Effective Ministries and Believers, call 800.943.6490 or visit www.JonasClark.com.

JONAS CLARK MINISTRIES

Biblical answers you've been searching for...

From the revolutionary teaching ministry of Jonas Clark,
Topics written with you in mind including, apostolic and prophetic issues,
deliverance, healing and Spirit-led living. Great for your library or a gift for
pastors, teachers and students of the Word.

30 PIECES OF SILVER
Discerning religious spirits and entering the Kingdom.

ISBN 1-116885-18-4

JEZEBEL: Seducing Goddess of War
Recognize this spirit's manipulative ways and break free from its controlling powers.

ISBN 1-886885-04-4

EXPOSING SPIRITUAL WITCHCRAFT
How to overcome curses, demons, witchcraft and controlling powers.

ISBN 1-886885-00-1

LIFE AFTER REJECTION:
God's path to emotional healing. Start prospering over rejection and reclaim your life from fear.

ISBN 1-886885-22-2

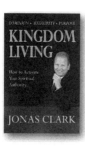

KINGDOM LIVING
How to activate your spiritual authority
Discover dominion restoration and purpose in the Kingdom of God.

ISBN 1-886885-21-4

EFFECTIVE MINISTRIES AND BELIEVERS
Introducing the apostolic ministry and what it means to you.

ISBN 1-886885-25-7